FINDING GRACE
in my process

FINDING GRACE
in my process

KYLA ESTIVERNE

Copyright © 2024 by Kyla Estiverne

2nd Edition

All rights reserved. This book or any portion thereof may not be reproduced or used in any manner whatsoever without the express written permission of the publisher except for the use of brief quotations in a book review.

Limits of Liability and Disclaimer of Warranty

The author and publisher shall not be liable for your misuse of this material. This book is strictly for informational purposes. The purpose of this book is to educate and entertain. The author and publisher do not guarantee anyone following these techniques, suggestions, tips, ideas, or strategies will become successful. The author and publisher shall have neither liability nor responsibility to anyone with respect to any loss or damage caused, or alleged to be caused, directly or indirectly by the information contained in this book. Views expressed in this publication do not necessarily reflect the views of the publisher.

This is a work of creative nonfiction. The events are portrayed to the best of Kyla Estiverne's memory and knowledge. While all the stories in this book are true, some names and identifying details have been changed to protect the privacy of the people involved.

Cover Design: by Triv ilovedesignsbytriv@gmail.com

Printed in the United States of America
Keen Vision Publishing, LLC
www.publishwithKVP.com
ISBN: 978-1-955316-61-3

Dedicated to everyone who has experienced any type of hardship in their lives. May this book remind you of God's love for you. There is grace in the process.

Contents

INTRODUCTION	9
MESSY BEGINNINGS	11
MISTREATED	19
MOLESTED	27
GOD'S GOODNESS	33
DIVINE SHIFTS	41
THANKFUL FOR THE RAIN	47
PROMISE-KEEPING GOD	53
MEET THE AUTHOR	57
STAY CONNECTED	59

Introduction

The book you are holding was penned to encourage people of every gender, race, nationality, age, and religion. It was written to honor the promise of God and show the beautiful power of God's grace. Though it details many painful memories, I did not write this book to offend or bring shame to anyone but to testify of God's saving power. As you journey through each page, you will read about how a child who endured many trials now stands not as a victim but as an overcomer.

I often sit and think about all God has allowed me to survive. One day, as I sat in gratitude, I wondered how I could glorify God and share my testimony in a way that would draw others close to Him. He placed the idea for this book in my heart. There is nothing I can ever do to repay God for all He has done and continues to do for me. However, this book is my way of sharing His goodness with the world.

FINDING GRACE IN MY PROCESS

Though this memoir details the story of my life, I pray that after reading this book, you are encouraged to press through whatever difficulties you have faced or may be facing. I pray that my testimony leads you directly to The Man who died and gave His life on the cross just for you. I pray it challenges you to give God another yes, despite what your life has been like. I pray it opens the door to your healing and breakthrough. More than anything, I pray this book helps you develop a deeper appreciation and gratitude for our Heavenly Father.

Messy Beginnings

Where did it all begin? Well, that depends on who is telling the story. For 22 years, my grandmother told me that my mother could not take care of my five siblings and me. I have four brothers and a sister. My sister and I are fraternal twins. A little after my twin sister and I were born, my mother would drop me off at my grandmother's (who was my mom's dad's girlfriend, aka my mom's stepmom...*let's call her Mary*) to babysit me. Then, when I was seven months, my mother decided that she did not want me anymore. So, as the story goes, she dropped me off at Mary's house with a sugar water bottle and a dirty, taped diaper. Mary took me in, brought me clothes, and raised me as her very own. According to Mary and her daughter (whom we will call, Nadege) my mother promised to return to get me when she got back on her feet, but she never did. Apparently, after many years, she returned, but Mary refused to give me back to my mother because she loved me so much.

Growing up, I heard this story often and believed every word of it. Mary would tell this story to all her friends and family. I felt like an orphan, unwanted, and not good enough for anyone. I could not understand why Mary had to tell everybody that my mom did not want me. She made me feel like leftovers; I was just there because I had no other option.

While writing this book, I learned the true story. As I gathered information from my family and other people who were around when I was younger, I discovered that the story Mary and Nadege told me for 22 years was a complete LIE. As a child, they manipulated me to make me think my mother never wanted me.

Here is what really happened.

My mother worked overtime to take care of my siblings and me. She would work for hours and hours at a time and, as a result, would often be exhausted. One day, she left my siblings and me at home with my brothers' father while she went to work. My brothers share a father, and my twin, my youngest brother, and I share a father.

We were supposed to be at home with my brothers' father, whom we will call David. Well, David decided to leave us home alone. The house was a mess. My mother worked crazy hours, and David just did not clean. There were empty beer bottles everywhere because David was and still is an alcoholic. The lights were disconnected. My mom would not give David the money to pay all the bills because he would use it for alcohol. There was also old food from takeout on the table, and the bed had no sheets on it.

Our home was not a safe environment for children. So, one of David's ex-girlfriends decided to call the cops. I feel as though she was trying to get back at my mom. I only wish she knew how much suffering her actions would cause six innocent children in the future. The police showed up, saw our environment, and took us into Child Protective Services (CPS). According to family members, I was about one at the time.

David's brother, whom we will call Paul, told my mother what happened and informed her that she needed to get to the police station. When she arrived, she was arrested and charged with Child Neglect- No Bodily Harm. My godmother tried to get custody but could not. My biological aunt also tried, but she could not because her husband was a felon. Finally, Mary learned what happened and decided she wanted to get me. Mary tried to get me and my twin sister, Kayla, but the judge felt Mary was too old to raise two little girls.

Before giving her custody, CPS checked Mary's house to ensure it was safe for a toddler. She passed the check, and the courts granted custody. Our biological father's sister got my twin sister, Kayla, but she did not want me. My three older brothers went to live with their father, and my youngest brother went across the world to live in Turks and Caicos with our aunt.

Does Anybody Want Me?

Growing up with my grandmother, I experienced a ton of psychological trauma. She would constantly tell me that my mother left me on her doorstep and that my mother did not want me. She reminded me of this at least once every month. I also heard things like, *"Girl, your parents never even brought a fifty-cent juice for you."* Whenever I asked my grandmother where my mother was or expressed a desire to see my mother, Mary would tell me that my mother was too busy and did not want me. My grandmother even told me that my mother was prostituting her body on the streets. Mary often told me that she was the only one who truly loved me. According to her, when CPS came, she was the only person willing to take me in.

These stories made me extremely sad. I could not understand how a mother could leave her child without any remorse. As you can imagine, hearing stories like this made me despise my mother.

Even when she did visit me, it was difficult to love her or believe anything she said. My mother often told me that she fought her hardest to get us all back since the day she lost us. She wanted her kids to live with her. I can recall when she promised me that she would win us back and live happily ever after. She also explained to me that she was very depressed, but she knew God would get her through. Despite what she said, all I heard in my head were my grandmother's stories. As a child, I did not know what to believe.

MESSY BEGINNINGS

I later learned that Mary gave my mother a hard time when she came to see me. When my mother was allowed to visit me, she would take me down the street from my house to a big church known as Saint Mary Church. We would sit and talk for hours. She would tell me how much she loved and wanted me, that she was working on getting a house. She explained that to get complete custody of all her children, she would need to have a home with at least five bedrooms and two bathrooms. There were six of us in total, and we would all need enough space.

After visits with my mother, I would be so happy and tell everyone that my mother was coming to get me and I would live with her. Mary would rain on my parade and tell me that none of it was true. There were times when months would go by without me seeing or hearing from my mother.

During these times, I stopped wanting to see my mother and preferred to stay with Mary. So many painful questions ran through my mind, like, *"Why wasn't I good enough? Why weren't my siblings and I good enough to be loved?"*

Being told so often that my mother and father did not want me caused me to hate my parents and lose total respect for them. Growing up, I believed I only had my grandmother. She was the only person I felt cared for me.

Even though I am very grateful for my grandmother, I experienced many trials while living with her — things a child should never have to deal with. In this book, I will discuss those things to help you understand my upbringing, the mistakes I made, but most importantly, how God allowed me to triumph over every circumstance. The purpose of this book is not to bring shame to the people in my childhood or me, but to bring glory to God and let the world know that God has the power to turn trials into victory.

The Power of Forgiveness

Writing this book has led to my deliverance in Jesus and has helped me forgive everyone who had a hand in my difficult upbringing. I respect that my grandmother tried her hardest to raise me well, but the truth remains that many of the things I endured in her household caused me psychological trauma that took me years to heal from. I am still on my journey to healing, but one of the biggest factors has been forgiveness.

Throughout my healing process, I have learned the power and benefits of forgiveness. I am only able to tell my story and help others today because of the power of forgiveness. We often think forgiveness is about letting the other person get away with the hurt or pain they caused, but forgiveness is deeper than that. It is about allowing yourself to be free. It is about living in peace.

When someone hurts you, you spend a lot of time replaying their words or actions in your mind. As a result, you hold yourself in bondage to what they did. Before long, you start to believe what they said or even that you deserved what they did to you. This leads to being fearful of reaching the goals God has set for you.

After forgiving my family, my eyes were opened to the truth of who I was in God. Even though I wanted to hold on to the pain and the hurt of what they said and did to me, I felt much lighter when I decided to let it go.

God desires us to love one another like Christ loves the church. The church is the people of God. Christ loved us so much that He laid down His life for us. He did not wait until we were perfect to love us. Instead, he loved us and died for us while we were still in sin.

We do things that disappoint God every day, but He does not give us what we deserve for our sins. Instead, He loves us and forgives us. God does this so that we will have an example of how to love each other. Forgiving my family freed me and taught me how to love the way God has instructed us to love.

As you read my story and learn about the things I endured, you may wonder, *"How in the world did she forgive them for this?"* It was truly the love and conviction of God that allowed me to forgive those who caused me so much heartache. I pray that you will be encouraged to do the same and begin your healing journey.

Mistreated

Now that you know a little about how my life story began, let's talk about my childhood. I grew up in Miami, Florida, in a small, well-known city called Little Haiti. The household I was raised in had four bedrooms and one bathroom. My grandmother and I shared this household with two other families. About fifteen people lived in our house. I was raised with nine other children. One of the children in the household became my best friend; we did everything together. Her name was Sunshine.

Sunshine's father would always visit and pick her up, and he would usually take me if Mary allowed. I always thought Sunshine and I would someday move out and find our future, and we sure did. We experienced some dreadful times growing up. I remember getting beaten butt-naked for being in the shower too long. Mary and Nadege did not like us running the water too long; I guess it made the water bill too high. After these beatings, Mary would walk out of the bathroom, and Sunshine and I would turn to each other and laugh! We laughed hard and joked with each other about the facial reactions we made while getting a beating. I guess that was just a coping method of ours. Sunshine was often teased by Mary, Nadege, and the other kids in the house. They would call her 'Monkey' and talk about her skin, but I always thought she was beautiful. Sunshine became the sister I always wanted.

Mary had a goody closet, and we felt that if you were not her biological grandchildren, you could not go inside. She had a lock on the door and allowed her grandchildren to open it whenever they wanted. On good days, Sunshine and I were able to get goodies. The difference in how Mary treated all of the children was apparent. We did not understand why she treated us so badly.

Being raised without my twin sister and siblings was tough, but Sunshine always made it easier. We would catch the bus to the mall. We would play in the rain with the other children and, of course, I would get a beating after. I got beat so much that I did not care. Those moments of fun were worth it for me. Sunshine's mother lived in the house as well, so she got away with some things and missed a few beatings when her mother was around.

On Sundays, my grandmother would go to church. I was raised as Catholic. Being raised Catholic meant we attended church on Sundays and Saturdays. Saturday services consisted of going to a catholic school. In these classes, they prepped us for communion. On Sunday, we would do communion; bread and wine were consecrated and shared. We would get into a line, and one by one, we would receive the bread from the priest and drink wine from the same cup. He would wipe the cup with a cloth, and then the next person would go. As I got older and gave this some thought, it was very disgusting to consider all the backwash in the cup from each individual, young and old. After taking communion, we walked back to our seats, got on our knees, and prayed. We were not allowed to talk.

I hated attending Catholic church because I felt like it was boring, but Mary would always say, *"You better come on and go to church with you. You know Nadege will find a reason to beat you."* She was right.

If you can recall, Nadege was Mary's daughter, my aunt. She treated me worse than anyone. Nadege always found a reason to talk down or beat me. I can recall being sick with the stomach virus for a couple of days. My grandmother, Mary, tried to whip up many home remedies, but nothing worked. I vomited and had diarrhea for days; it was horrible. I was too sick to go to church with my grandmother that Sunday morning, so I stayed at home with Nadege. Nadege made some eggs for breakfast, but I could not eat because I was so weak and nauseous. Well, she beat me and said things like, *"You are going to eat this food!"* but I literally could not eat or hold anything down.

While she beat me, I started to vomit, but she did

not stop at all. I remember crying my eyes out as my little body slipped through the vomit, trying to get up. Later that day, Mary came home, and I told her everything. Nadege's husband suggested they take me to the hospital, and they did. On my way out the door, Grandma Mary whispered to me, "Do not tell them I gave you any remedies. They might take you to another home or put me in jail."

When I got to the hospital, I did not tell them anything. After running tests, the doctors confirmed that I had a stomach virus, prescribed me Pepto Bismol, and said I needed to allow the virus to run its course.

Where Is The Love?

The hatred I felt from Nadege was so painful. She and my mom were raised together as sisters. Growing up, they had a very complicated relationship. I do not know why, and there are so many untold stories of what happened between the two of them. When they became adults, the hatred between them grew even more. I believe this had a lot to do with how Nadege treated me. She would always say, *"You are just like your mother: STUPID."* These words always came to mind when I tried to accomplished things growing up. Whatever the reason, being treated so differently by her and my grandmother made me feel hopeless. I started to think Nadege was right about me. Maybe I was stupid. Maybe that's why my mother did not want me. These thoughts robbed my mind my entire childhood. It was bad enough that I did not have my mother and father. The two women who should have built my confidence and spoke life into me killed me mentally. I felt like I had died before I really started living. As I look back on it, it was like I had experienced an emotional death that only Jesus could resurrect me from.

As a child, I wondered why I did not have the life and love that other children had. I would look into the crowd at school events, searching for a familiar face cheering me on, but no one was there for me. Though I loved my Grandma Mary, I knew that kids were supposed to have mothers and fathers. Even though I did not have a loving environment, I knew that kids were supposed to be treated better than I was being treated. I could not understand why I did not have those things.

The lack of emotional and mental support in my household started to weigh on me heavily when I was in elementary school. One day, while arguing with one of the children in the household, she began to call me an orphan. No one had ever called me that before, but I had heard the word on TV and read it in books. It rang a million times in my head before the tears began running down my face. I did not realize I was crying until I heard Sunshine say to the girl, "Why would you say that? You made her cry."

My heart began to beat slowly, and it felt like the world was closing in around me. *"Orphan?"* I thought to myself. *"Am I really an orphan?"* The more I thought about it, the more I realized how much I fit the description. I lived at home with people who were not my biological family. I did not have my mom, dad, or siblings. I was given away (or so I thought at the time.) As these thoughts sunk in, I started to question why I was even alive. Before I knew it, I was ready to end it all. I decided to kill myself. I did not see a reason to continue the life I had.

I walked to the kitchen, grabbed a butter knife, hid on the side of the house, and planned to stab myself. Yeah, I know now that a butter knife would not have caused much damage, but in my little mind, I thought it would work. Grandma Mary caught me, and I yelled over and over, "I am going to kill myself!" She grabbed the butter knife, spanked me with her hand, and told me never to do that again.

Later that day, I told my grandmother why I had tried to kill myself and what the little girl called me, but she did not say anything.

Thankfully, God knew what I needed. When Sunshine's dad found out about what had happened, he stood up for me and handled the situation. After I accepted Christ into my life and learned how to understand scriptures in the Bible, I found many about orphans. James 1:27 says, *"The worship that God wants is this: caring for orphans or widows who need help and keeping yourself free from the world's evil influence. This is the kind of worship that God accepts as pure and good."*

This scripture made me appreciate Sunshine's

father for taking a stand for me. Even though my grandmother and aunt caused me much trauma, they also worshipped God by taking me in and caring for me when my mother could not. All of this showed me that despite what I went through, God had sent people into my life to care for me. Even though the world may have classified me as an orphan, I have never been an orphan. Psalm 68:5 lets me know that God is a father to the fatherless and motherless. Through good days and bad days, I always had a parent in God. Even when I wonder why I was treated so badly, I remember that sometimes, it rains on the just and the unjust. (Matthew 5:45). God's word has helped me to heal from so many of the things I have endured. Learning more about God and allowing His love into my heart has filled every emptiness I have ever felt. If you get nothing else from this book, know that God can be anything and everything you need. He is omnipresent, which means that He is wherever you need Him to be. All you have to do is ask and allow Him in.

Molested

Unfortunately, being beat, mistreated, and emotionally abused was not all I experienced as a child. Mary sold beers out of her household to make extra cash. There were often a lot of men going in and out of the house. One man in particular, *whom we will call Lucas*, took a special interest in Sunshine and me. He would come over, have a few drinks, and then ask me to sit on his lap. I thought nothing of it because I thought he was a family friend. He would rub my back and then ask me for a kiss. When I reached out to kiss him, he would stick his tongue in my mouth.

The Haitian culture has something called "Sileh," which means to greet someone with a kiss on the cheek. So, at that age, I thought what Lucas did was okay. Even though it felt weird, I decided not to tell anyone except Sunshine. When I told her, she shared that she had experienced the same thing with Lucas. Sometimes, it feels like it was just yesterday. Even though Lucas is deceased, I can still feel his slimy saliva intertwining with mines and his hot, extra-large hand rubbing up and down my back to my butt.

Each time, I would pull away and think to myself, *"This cannot be right."* Due to the abuse I experienced from Nadege, I was too afraid that no one would believe me if I told them. As I shared before, Nadege would often find any reason to "discipline" me. I felt like if I told her, she would have beaten and blamed me. It is sad, but the wedge between us made me feel like I could not tell anyone I had been molested. I carried the guilt and dirtiness alone for years.

Unfortunately, this was not the only time I experienced molestation. One day, I came home from school, and Grandma Mary and Nadege were away at the store. An old man, *whom we will call Pierre*, lived in the spare room with Mary's husband. When Pierre realized I was home from school, he told me to sit in his room on his bed until my grandmother got home. So, I did. I thought to myself, *"Why not? Pierre is my grandmother's good friend."* After a while, I started to feel uncomfortable and unsafe. I decided to leave and watch TV in Mary's room until she got back. Pierre did not agree with that. Before I could get to the door, he threw my body to the floor, got on top of me, and proceeded to remove my pants.

I tried to kick him off, but he was too heavy. Then, I heard a car alarm, like someone locking their car doors. It was Mary and Nadege, and they were right on time. Pierre released me in fear, and I ran to Mary's room. When Mary saw me, I was still trembling from being scared. I could not even get the words out to tell her, and she did not ask me anything. I was so hurt. I wondered, *"Can she not see the fear in my eyes? Why can't she see that something is different about me?"* I wanted to tell her, but I was just too afraid. I could not comprehend what had happened. Feeling uncertain and as if I had done something wrong caused me to keep the details of the molestation to myself.

When I turned 22, I called Nadege to ask her where Lucas lived. She told me that he had passed away in Haiti. Then, she asked me why I was looking for him. Though I was afraid, I took a deep breath and told her what he did to me. After explaining the situation, the other end of the phone went silent for a few minutes. Nadege finally replied and said, "You should have been said something. He's dead and gone now. What am I supposed to do about that?"

My heart sunk hearing those words. I thought she would apologize, but she did not. I thought she would realize that she physically and emotionally abused me so much that I was afraid to say anything. None of this happened. I replied, "Okay," and hung up the phone. I definitely did not tell her what Pierre had done. A few months after that conversation with Nadege, Pierre moved out and later passed away.

Over time, carrying the secret of being molested destroyed my spiritual, mental, emotional, and even physical health. As I grew older, my perception of men got worse. My father, the man who was supposed to show me how to be treated by men, was incarcerated. The molestation was the first male attention and touch I received, and it made me feel even more negative about interacting with me. By the time I made it to high school, I despised men. I felt as though they had nothing to offer but trouble. Unfortunately, this did not keep me away from men. It only led me to the wrong kind of men. I dealt with men who did not respect me, lied to me, cheated on me, and further proved what I believed to be true about men. Some of the guys I dated even tried to pressure me into having sex with them. I really wanted to do it, to please them and give them what I felt they deserved for being with me, but I could not. I would do other sexual things to keep them from leaving me, but I could never go through with sexual intercourse. When I got older, I started going through counseling. During one of my therapy sessions, I realized that my fear of being intimate with men strung from my perception of men and the molestations.

God's Perfect Love

When a man named Jesus came into my life, my entire perspective about men shifted. It was the first time in my life that I experienced a true man's love. I learned that Jesus loves me and wants nothing in exchange for the love He gives. In John 15: 9, Jesus says, *"As the Father has loved me, so have I loved you. Abide in my love."* At first, it was so hard for me to interpret Jesus' love for me. But, by faith, I received

His love. His love has been there for me on days when I did not act like I belonged to God. His love has been there for me on gloomy days and days when I sinned. Despite my actions, present and past, Jesus' love has been consistent. His love teaches me faithfulness and righteousness all at the same time. 1 John 1:9 says, *"If we confess our sins, he is faithful and just and will forgive us our sins and purify us from all unrighteousness."* As a byproduct of Jesus' love for us, when we mess up, we can still come to Him, tell Him what we have done, and being the faithful and righteous Father that He is, He patches us up and makes us new again.

God never says, *"This is the last time I'll put you back together again."* When I come before Him to repent, He forgives me and reminds me that I am His. I owe Him my life.

Before I received God's love, I never thought I would meet a man who would love me and care for me. Honestly, even if I did, I would have been too afraid to let him in. Now, because of the love of God, I know what to expect from a man. God's love is the perfect example of how a man should love me. Through my healing process, I am learning how to accept and respond to that kind of love. I believe that I am deserving of that love, and in God's timing, I believe I will receive it.

It is hard to receive the love of others or even love others without first experiencing God's love. I am grateful that no matter who comes and goes, God's love for me is forever.

God's Goodness

As I mentioned before, my father spent a lot of time in jail when I was growing up. He was arrested plenty of times. He was charged in 2003, spent six years in jail, and was released in 2009. Shortly after that, he was arrested several times again and was back in jail. My father was always a warden of state custody when my siblings and I were removed from my mother's home. In my opinion, he did not seem to care as much. I guess his circumstances did not allow him to do too much. I recall when he was released from prison. He rarely checked in on me, and when he did come to visit, I was so attached to Grandma Mary that I did not want to spend a night out without her. When he picked me up, I would spend some time with him, then cry and beg him to take me home. That was basically our relationship when I was growing up.

As for my mother, she really was fighting hard to

gain custody of my siblings and me. I was not aware at the time, but while I was in elementary school, she took parental classes and searched relentlessly for a home so that the courts would award her full custody again.

Even though both of my parents were fighting their own battles, I needed them more than ever at this time in my life. I was never a bad student, but around 3rd grade, I would do things to get in trouble. Though this did not happen often, I needed guidance and support to stay on the right path. Thankfully, God put me on the hearts of a few teachers, and they made a great and positive impact on my life. There were two teachers, Ms. Mitchell and Ms. A, who impacted me most. I will forever be grateful for them.

Ms. A came into my life when I was older, but Ms. Mitchell impacted me most in elementary school. She hosted an after-school program called Heat Academy. Heat Academy was funded by the Miami Heat Basketball team and allowed students the opportunity to go on field trips and have access to tutoring and mentorship. It was a great program, and I was blessed to have been a part of it. Ms. Mitchell and I would always sit down and talk; I felt comfortable venting and sharing my heart with her. She always listened, showed that she cared, and gave me wise advice.

On the day of my 5th-grade graduation, my aunt Nadege was running late from work, so I had no transportation to graduation. After all, I had gone through to make it through elementary school, and graduation meant a lot to me. I could not miss it. So, I called Ms. Mitchell. Without hesitation, she picked me up and gave me a ride to my fifth-grade graduation. I was always grateful for her.

If you are reading this and you are a teacher, know that you are appreciated. You are essential to the future of every child you are blessed to teach. I pray God gives you the strength to always create a safe place for your students to share their hearts and the thoughts in their minds. Your willingness to be there for your students beyond curriculum could be the very thing that saves their lives. It saved mine...

A Dream Come True?

By this point, I know you may be wondering if my mother was ever successful in getting full custody of my siblings and me. Well, let's just say it was a difficult journey. Court date after court date, judges would turn my mother away with a longer list of things she needed to complete to win full custody. Nevertheless, she did not give up. Finally, on August 11, 2008, my mother, Ketly Estiverne, won full custody of all six of her children.

That had to have been the happiest day of my life. We were all so excited to finally be living together again. What was it like to finally be under the same roof with my mother and siblings? It was everything to me, but it did come with many struggles. We were apart for very long, so it took some major adjustments. We all had to learn each other and learn how to love each other. My mother did not have the best jobs, but she worked hard to keep a roof over our heads, clothes on our backs, and food in our bellies. On days when my mom did not have money to feed us, she would fry dough with sugar so we could have something warm to eat—being without taught us how to be creative.

    I grew very close to my mother, and she became my best friend. I would listen to her, and she would share everything that was in her heart and mind. My mother spent years apologizing for what had happened to us while she was away. She also continuously apologized when she could not provide for us. There were days when my mother would just sit and cry because she could not take care of us the way she wanted because she did not have the money. She became depressed and tired. She often felt guilty for getting custody of us. My mother felt like she was not giving us the lives we deserved or making up for the lost time. I never blamed my mom for the struggles we went through with her. She did the best she could, and she did what she knew was best. I did not expect her to go and steal out of a store to feed us. I made an oath that one day, I would be able to take care of her, and she would never go another day hungry or lacking anything.

    My mother has always been a woman of faith. She has been serving God for as long as I can remember. Watching my mom serve God relentlessly made me want to get to know God for myself. I started attending church with my friend, Ashley, and my love for God grew so strong. Ashley and I would always find transportation to church, whether the church bus, metro bus, or just catching a ride with someone who attended the church. Ashley and I went to every service and rarely missed. That church was where I first encountered the Holy Spirit. It was where I first started hearing God's voice and the place where I gave God my first yes! I attended this church for about four years. The people I met at church were not my friends; they were family. Even though I had a strong desire for God, it was always easy to stay on the right path. I struggled with my faith a lot. Nevertheless, I wanted to be closer to God, so I fought to stay the course.

He Gave Me A Testimony

In 2013, when I was fifteen years old, I started experiencing major headaches nearly eight hours a day. It had gotten so bad that I stopped functioning. I could not eat or talk; everything caused my headaches to get worse. One day, I was rushed to Joe DiMaggio Children Hospital, located in Hollywood, Florida. I went into an emergency procedure called a Lumbar Puncture, also know as Spinal Tab. This procedure removes fluid from the spine in the lower back through a hollow needle, usually for diagnostic purposes. After testing the fluid in my spine, the doctors were shocked at how high the pressure of my fluid was; they could not understand how I was still able to see perfectly fine. I was admitted and diagnosed with Pseudotumor Cerebri, a condition in which the pressure around your brain increases, causing headaches and vision problems. It was also known as a "false brain tumor" because its symptoms are like those caused by brain tumors. The pressure in my skull was increasing for no obvious reason. The doctors explained to my mother and me that I could possibly go blind or have a brain aneurysm and die instantly. I ended up receiving two Lumbar Punctures.

I was in the hospital for a week, and I cried every day. I just wanted to go home. The nurses often came into my room throughout the night, checking my eyes to ensure I had not gone blind and pricking my finger to monitor my dangerously high sugar levels. During the day, I constantly had MRIs and X-rays. I wanted more than anything for my life to go back to normal. The only thing I could do was worship. So I would play gospel music in my room and worship God every chance I got.

Though this was a difficult time in my life, I am grateful that it taught me that God is truly a healer. No one can ever make me doubt that. I walked out of that hospital with eyes that could see, limbs that could move, and free of headaches.

I do not serve or praise God because of what I hear people say or testify. I have my testimony of His goodness, grace, and mercy. He did not have to, but He proved Himself to me. He has never failed me. He never will. I know Him to be a faithful God, a Man of His word. There is nothing more beautiful than experiencing God for yourself. When you think about everything you have endured and gone through, I pray you can see your testimony of God's goodness and faithfulness to His promises. That testimony has the power to encourage you in dark days and even empower others to keep the faith. The Bible says that they overcame by the blood of the Lamb and the word of their testimony. For a long time, I hated the life I was given. I did not understand why so many bad things happened to me. Now, I understand that God was developing me and building my testimony. Whatever your testimony is, do not be ashamed of it! Instead, allow it to push you and others closer to God.

Divine Shifts

In the 10th grade, I met a teacher who changed my perspective on life. Her name was Ms. Opia Astwood, also known as Ms. A. She became my listening ear, the one I could run to no matter the situation. She took me in and did as much as she could to be there for me. She introduced me to her family, and they accepted me with no restraints. Ms. A's mother accepted me with open arms and called me her bonus grandbaby. The feelings of warmth and safety I felt around her and her family were like nothing I had ever experienced before.

The truth is, when I first met Ms. A, I tried to make her life a living hell. Or, so I thought. I would misbehave in her class horribly and even encouraged my friends to join me. No matter what I did, she remained humble and always extended love. Her response confused me. *Why won't she just kick me out of this class?* I often wondered. Other teachers would have sent me straight to the principal's office, but Ms. Astwood took me in. At first, this was not comforting. It actually frustrated me. *"How could she love "collateral damage"? How could she care for someone like me? This woman must be nuts to love me,"* I thought to myself.

Beyond my confusion and frustration with her, God knew just what I needed. I believe He gave her the patience and the grace to deal with me. Her love, kindness, and understanding began breaking down the tall walls of abandonment, rejection, and confusion that I had built around my heart. Before meeting her, I did not think anyone could get in.

I eventually stopped resisting her and allowed her into my world. She helped me with school assignments and even guided me through the process of enrolling in college. After school, we would talk about my life goals. Ms. A believed I could be great and was committed to helping me achieve. She did not want anything in exchange.

Ms. A's support showed me just how much God loved me. To this day, I do not know what she may have been going through in her personal life. Nevertheless, God disrupted her life and assigned her to impact my life. She accepted and embraced me with a pure heart. Her influence changed the direction of my life, and I began my journey to more healing, deliverance, and freedom.

It Hurts So Good

Someone once told me, "Ky, I think you are addicted to pain. I think you like the way it feels. It is like an attraction to you". Their statement made me upset. I did not think it was true. When I looked at the decisions I made, I realized they were right. I had a real problem.

Sometimes I did things that could have cost me my life or serious injuries. I did not care. I knew my behavior was not normal or acceptable, but I was addicted to suffering. I was addicted to toxicity. I could not see that because I had spent most of my life blaming others for everything that had transpired in my life. Placing the blame on others justified my actions; I did not have to be accountable for making the changes I wanted to see in my life.

Before realizing I was addicted to pain, I struggled with homosexuality and lusted after older women who were already established. I was on a search for love and acceptance in all the wrong places. I desired the love and affection I did not receive as a child and thought these women could help me heal. Most of them were already in serious relationships, and my dealings with them nearly got me killed.

Until I recognized my addiction to pain, I was often in a dark mental space; I did not want anything good for myself. I only felt alive when I got in trouble or near-death experienced. One time, I recall being so depressed that I almost jumped out of the car on the highway while a friend of mine was driving. When we finally got to our destination, I begged her not to leave me alone. Thoughts of suicide flooded my mind, and I knew I would end it all that day. Death knocked at my door, and I wanted to let it in. Voices of negativity screamed in my head. That day, I needed someone to sit and talk with me. As I pleaded with my friend to stay with me, she looked at me and said, "Ky, I just do not know how to help you. I have to leave and take care of my children." With that, she left me in my car.

I was about thirty minutes away from home. I got on the highway and preceded to speed. Tears ran down my face, and I prayed that I would swerve out of control and die. Suddenly, my phone rang, and it was one of my teachers. She told me to meet her in a parking lot. Once I got there, we talked for hours. Something broke off me that day. The heaviness of suicide lifted off me.

With the help of Jesus, I realized that it was time for a change. The change would have to begin with me. I had to take responsibility for my life. Yes, awful things happened to me. No, I could not avoid them. Yes, it was my guardian's duty to keep me safe. However, it was time for me to be accountable for my future.

The Journey Begins

I did not know what to do to get myself out of the hole I was in, but I trusted God, and He walked with me through my process. After disappointing so many people and having individuals walk out of my life, I did not know how to trust God. Whenever I made mistakes, I was so afraid that He would be done with me as well. Psalm 51:7 says, *"The sacrifices of God are a broken spirit: A broken and a contrite heart, O God, thou wilt not despise."* Those words assured me that God would never walk away from me. He always knew what to do. He always had a ram in the bush for me, and He never treated me as my sin deserved. As I thought about God's faithfulness to me despite me, it did not make sense not to give my life to him completely.

When I decided to commit to my process, serve God and allow Him to heal me, I had to give up the life of homosexuality, my addiction to pain, unforgiveness, and many other things. It has not been easy, but it has been worth it. Exiting my old lifestyle required daily submission and a lot of heart work. I had to make some tough decisions and still do. Am I perfect? Not at all. I still mess up. But every time I fall, God gives me the strength to stand up again, forgive myself, and move closer to righteousness.

This process would be impossible without God's grace. When I am weak, he is strong. Apostle Paul says in Philippians 3:12-15, *"Not that I have already obtained this or am already perfect, but I press on to make it my own because Christ Jesus has made me his own. Brothers, I do not consider that I have made it my own. But one thing I do: forgetting what lies behind and straining forward to what lies ahead, I press on toward the goal for the prize of the upward call of God in Christ Jesus. Let those of us who are mature think this way, and if in anything you think otherwise, God will reveal that also to you."* I meditate on these scriptures any time I fall short. It encourages me to keep moving forward.

Philippians 1:6 reminds us, *"I am sure that the good work God began in me will continue until he completes it on the day when Jesus Christ comes again."* God is committed to perfecting us. All we need to do is receive His grace and stay the course.

Thankful for the Rain

After I graduated from high school, I enrolled in Concordia College in Selma, AL. It was not easy to move away from my entire family, but I wanted to make my mother proud. It was challenging to adjust to a new area, but I tried my best to make it work. I joined the band, and one of the band leads would bully me severely. I guess that was the thing for black college bands, but I did not like it at all. One day, she looked at me and said, "You look like you have down syndrome." Others laughed, but I did not find her statement funny. I could not understand why someone would joke about something so severe or why she felt the need to pick on me. She did not know my life story or how hard I was trying to get out of a very dark place. Over time, I began to have suicidal thoughts again and become extremely depressed. I missed my family. I missed being happy. I did the only thing I knew to do. I dropped out of college and went back home.

A few months after I returned to Florida, my family and I were evicted out of our home. This resulted in all of us living in different locations...again. I moved back with Grandma Mary, got two jobs, and enrolled in Asa College. In the morning, I attended class, after school, I worked at Footlocker, and overnight, I worked at Seven-eleven. I was often exhausted and barely able to hold on.

Homeless

One day, things got bad, and I decided to move out of Grandma Mary's house. I packed all my things and lived out of my car. It was like carrying my entire life with me everywhere I went. My car became my safe place. I stayed at people's houses here and there, but I never had a permanent location. I lived with my family often, but I spent a good amount of time at my best friend's house. Over time, I preferred to live out my car. It was more peaceful, and it belonged to me. I worked two jobs to keep it.

Being homeless was very difficult. I recall not having food to eat at times or only being able to afford something off the dollar menu at Mcdonald's. I constantly prayed to God for a way out. My mother's biological mother, Grandma Floraine, also welcomed me into her home when I needed a break from living in my car. She made sure I had food to eat, encouraged me, and remained in God's, praying face for me. I am positive that the things I am blessed with now are because of her sincere prayers to God on my behalf.

During this time, I did not go to church as often. Before I dropped out of college, my mother and someone I looked up to spiritually got into a very heated argument. This individual said, "That is why Kyla is going to be pregnant, and she's never going to be s***." I carried the hurt those words caused me for years. I stopped going to church and even stopped praying. I could not believe the person I looked up to and often spoke into my life said those awful things about me. A part of me felt like this is what God was all about and that maybe God felt the same way about me. After that situation, anger and anxiety set in. I was angry at God and the individual. I went on a mission to prove them both wrong about me. I wanted to prove that I did not need him or God to be successful. When things continuously got worse, I blamed God. It started to feel like God only wanted me to suffer.

I'm Over It!

I got to a point where I was tired of trying. I was tired of church and God. I wanted no parts of anything dealing with faith. It started to feel like I had set my expectations too high. I expected too much from God, others, and even myself. For years, I blamed myself and refused to seek God. If you know anything about God, you know that even when you want to throw in the towel, He will not let you. Despite how far I had walked away from Him, He was still faithful to me. God began to deal with my heart about forgiveness. He also allowed me to see that in everything I was doing, I never put Him first, and I viewed Him through the eyes of others. As a result, I was not where I desired to be in life.

The Bible says in Proverbs 12:25, *"Anxiety in a man's heart weighs him down, but a good word makes him glad."* For years I had held so much anger towards this man and God, and it weighed me down. I was tired of doing things my way and finally surrendered and found my way back in God's arms. He embraced me as if I had never left.

Life is hard, but it is extremely difficult when we try to live it without God. I learned the hard way to depend on God solely. During my season of rebellion and unforgiveness, I made my life harder than it had to be, but God was still faithful to me. As I leaned back into prayer and reading the word, I started to realize that life would never be perfect. We will go through storms, trials, ups, and downs. Some of the things I had experienced as a young adult were just a part of adjusting into adulthood. When I stopped looking at my experiences like a punishment from God, I could see how God allowed these things to make me better. My struggles taught me how to budget and remain humble. Throughout my difficulty, I experienced the heart of God's people. I made so many friends that I would have never met and got support from those who could see my heart despite my situation. I learned how to sit in a storm and learn from it instead of leaving and getting defeated. I learned the power in praying,

"God, I may not be able to get out of this situation, but give me the peace and strength I need to get through it."

You might not believe this, but I would not trade my journey for anything. When I think about the peace and financial breakthrough I have now, I would go through it all over again. I believe that if God brings me to it, He can and will bring me through it.

I Choose Freedom

During a counseling session, my therapist once said, "The pen is in your hands, Ky. You get to write your life out now." I realized right then, and there it was totally up to me to heal and find healthy coping mechanisms for when I faced difficulty.

I decided that my freedom, peace, and health were too expensive to lose, so I chose to forgive. I forgave everyone that let me down, hurt me, spoke badly against me, or wronged me. I do not hold a grudge against my grandmother for the lies or even my aunt for the abuse. It all made me stronger. I am the woman of God that I am today because of it. The growth I am experiencing was worth every tear. I even forgave the spiritual leader that spoke ill of me. We reconciled, forgave each other, and even to this day, he still prays for and encourages me.

Now, I view the world, people, and places in a different way. I choose the relationships I want to have. I choose when to walk away from people who disrupt my peace. Instead of blaming others, I take full responsibility for my past, present, and future actions.

FINDING GRACE IN MY PROCESS

I no longer cry or complain about the hard life I once had. I learned things in my lows that my highs could never teach me. The greatest lesson was letting God lead my life. For so long, I fought with God and demanded things my way. When things did not go as I planned, I could not understand why. My lack of submission to God made my life a living hell, but God still did not leave me. Instead, he allowed life to humble me and show me that without Him, I am a ship without a sail. Since I began putting Him first in all things, my life took a beautiful turn.

Promise-Keeping God

When I think of my life's story, I am reminded of the story of Joseph in the book of Genesis. Joseph was the youngest of all his brothers and favored by God and his parents. His brothers grew jealous of him and wanted to kill him. Instead of killing him, they sold him into slavery. The traders took him into Egypt, where he worked as a slave, went through many trials, and ended up in prison. One day, King Pharaoh had a dream, and one of the former prisoners, who was then a servant of the King, remembered that Joseph could interpret dreams. Joseph interpreted King Pharaoh's dream and gained favor with the King. Joseph was made a ruler over many. During a time of famine, Joseph's brothers had to travel to Egypt to buy food. So much time had passed that they did not recognize the little brother they had sold into slavery. Nevertheless, Joseph recognized them and told them to take him to the entire family. Joseph forgave his brothers and blessed them and their entire families.

My experience and Joseph's experience teach me that when God says something, no man can stop what He has promised. After the trials, suffering, and lonely nights, I saw God's promises. I graduated college with an Associate's Degree in Criminal Justice. After graduating, I was hired as an Intake Clerk Bond Hearing Specialist. Within a year, I was promoted to lead worker within that unit. I was blessed with a new car, A 2016 Mazda 3. God even blessed me with stable housing. Over the last few years, I have not wanted for anything. God placed people in my life who did not have any impure motives; they just wanted to help me. I am forever grateful to each of them.

As I said in the introduction, I did not write this book to embarrass, expose, or bring shame to anyone. I wrote this book because I know what it is like to be on the brink of suicide and feel there is nothing left to live for. I know what it is like to be in the dark pits of life feeling helpless. In those seasons, I wish I would have had tangible proof that someone like me could become something great. I wrote this book to encourage everyone who reads it to keep pressing. The purpose of this book is to bring glory to God and give the world proof of His grace and faithfulness. I wrote this book so that others could learn of God's love and power. I wrote this book to tell the world about the God who wiped every tear from my eye, healed my brokenness, and brought me into His glorious light. I pray more than anything that this book has encouraged and uplifted you in whatever trials you may be facing.

It does not matter what your life looks like right now; God is not done with you. Yes, you have probably made some mistakes, but God can still turn your story around. I am living proof of it. I was once told by one of my spiritual counselors, Shemicka St Gerard, *"When God sees you, He sees His blood."* When God sees us, He is reminded that He loves us so much that He allowed His Son to die for our sin. So, He does not see your sin; He sees His child. Sometimes, we feel like we cannot go to God until we are perfect. But, here is the thing, you cannot get better without God. I know sometimes it feels like you cannot get right no matter how hard you try, but the purpose of the struggle is to keep you at God's feet. The purpose of your mistakes is to remind you that you need Jesus. He does not require you to be perfect before you come to Him. He just needs you to be willing and submitted.

The enemy enjoys making you think that God does not care or want you. He is a complete liar. God still wants you. He will always want you. His grace and mercy are enough to cover whatever you have done and whatever you have been through. I am an example of God's grace and saving power.

Believe me when I say God loves you despite whatever you have experienced. His love is greater than any pain that you are too afraid to talk about. His power can change any hellish situation you have endured. No matter the situation you may be facing right now, believe that our faithful God will never turn

His back on you. He can and will see you through.

Now, I have given you my testimony, but my story and encouragement alone cannot save you. So, before I close this book, I want to offer you the opportunity to receive Jesus Christ. If you want to experience God's hand in your life, you must receive Jesus Christ. You do not have to be in a physical church to accept Jesus Christ into your life. You can receive Jesus right where you are. The Bible says that this is all you have to do:

"That if you confess with your mouth, "Jesus is Lord," and believe in your heart that God raised him from the dead, you will be saved."

Romans 10:9

When you are ready, simply say this simple prayer:

"Dear Lord Jesus, I know that I am a sinner, and I ask for Your forgiveness. I believe You died for my sins and rose from the dead. I turn from my sins and invite You to come into my heart and life. I want to trust and follow You as my Lord and Savior."

That is it! You did it! Jesus says in Luke 15:10, *"I tell you, there is rejoicing in the presence of the angels of God over one sinner who repents."*

I am rejoicing with you! Congratulations on your salvation! May the rest of your days be the best of your days! Trust God and embrace His grace in your process.

Meet the Author

Kyla Estiverne is a first-time author who aspires to write for teens, young adults, and adults. Kyla works at Miami Dade State Attorney's Office in case screenings as a lead intake clerk worker. Her desire is to help people grow from pain and heartbreak. Through her healing journey, she learned the importance of putting God first in everything. She now dreams of helping others overcome molestation, pain, suffering, and heartbreak with God.

Her biggest accomplishment to date has been being the first in her family to publish a book at the age of twenty-three. Kyla Estiverne lives in Miami, FL and participates in church. She is growing in God, and loving those around her. To connect with Kyla Estiverne email Kylaestiverne@gmail.com

Stay Connected

Thank you for reading, *Finding Grace In My Process*. Kyla looks forward to connecting with you. Here are a few ways you can connect with the author.

INSTAGRAM   the.realky
FACEBOOK   Kyla Estiverne
EMAIL   kylaestiverne@gmail.com

www.ingramcontent.com/pod-product-compliance
Lightning Source LLC
Chambersburg PA
CBHW032100150426
43194CB00006B/600